Harold Spurgeon Paisley
Evangelist
1924 - 2015

'The Lord's Servant'

A Tribute by Dr Alastair Noble

ISBN-13: 978 1 910513 52 1

Copyright © 2016 by John Ritchie Ltd.
40 Beansburn, Kilmarnock, Scotland

www.ritchiechristianmedia.co.uk

All rights reserved. No part of this publication may be reproduced, stored in a retrievable system, or transmitted in any form or by any other means – electronic, mechanical, photocopy, recording or otherwise – without prior permission of the copyright owner.

Typeset by John Ritchie Ltd., Kilmarnock
Printed by CCB

Dedication
For my mother-in-law, Rosetta Paisley,
for her kindness and generosity over many years,
and
for my wife, Ruth, for her unfailing love and companionship

The Evangelist from Ballymena

Harold Spurgeon Paisley was born in Lurgan, Northern Ireland, on 27th May 1924. His middle name, after the great preacher of Victorian London, reflects the Baptist convictions of his parents. His wife, Rosetta ('Etta') Hagan, came from Gracehill, an old Moravian village near Ballymena. She was born on exactly the same day as her husband and for a time they attended the same school. They were married at Wellington St Gospel Hall, Ballymena, in 1946.

Harold was the eldest of the three children of Rev James Kyle and Isabella Paisley (nee Turnbull). James Kyle came originally from Sixmilecross, Co Tyrone; Isabella from Kilsyth, Scotland. After a period of ministry in Armagh, Rev Paisley became the pastor of Waveney Road Tabernacle in Ballymena. Harold's younger brother Ian became the Founder and Moderator of the Free Presbyterian Church of Ulster, the founder and Leader of the Democratic Unionist Party, First Minister of Northern Ireland, and, together with his wife Eileen, a member of the British House of Lords. His sister Margaret was a primary school teacher and wife of Rev James Beggs, the former minister of the large Free Presbyterian church in Ballymena.

Ballymena family c.1940

At the beginning of World War II, Harold left home and volunteered for service in the RAF as conscription did not apply in Northern Ireland. He quickly became a sergeant and rear air-gunner during the Battle of Britain. Few of those who flew with him survived the war. It emerged later, when a check of birth certificates was made, that he had been underage when he enrolled. He was then offered ground duties, but declined and was given an honourable discharge.

Sergeant in the RAF

While in London seeking further war service, Harold was shown great kindness by the family of a Baptist pastor whose brother, John Harper, was lost on the Titanic, and their Christian hospitality made a significant impression on him. He chose to join the Merchant Navy where he braved the hazards of the convoy system during the Battle of the North Atlantic and, on occasions, watched as similar ships were torpedoed by German U-boats. On his return to Northern Ireland towards the end of the war, he served for a time in the Royal Ulster Constabulary (RUC), but left after an angry dispute with a colleague.

The tumultous experiences of war service and the abrupt end to his police career had brought the ever-confident and somewhat reckless

> 'For God so loved the world that He gave His only begotten Son, that whosoever believeth in Him should not perish, but have everlasting life', John 3v16.
> - 'the source, scope, simplicity and solemnity of the Gospel'
> From Harold's messages

Harold to a low point in his life. Around this time, in 1944, while in Belfast, he experienced a dramatic conversion to Christ, after witnessing a road accident in which a man standing next to him was killed. Despite his dangerous war experiences, he was badly shaken by this incident, being violently and unexpectedly confronted with the reality of his mortality and the thought of eternity. He sought the counsel of Sergeant Murphy, a Christian with whom he had served in the RUC, and not long after was led to faith through the words of John 3 v16 which emphasises the need for repentance and a personal commitment to Jesus Christ. That verse was to become his favourite Bible text, and was almost always quoted when he preached. It was also the verse through which his wife Rosetta became a Christian in her early teens.

Within a relatively short time Harold immersed himself in evangelistic work, displaying early signs of being an effective preacher of the Gospel. It was a dramatic turn-around in his life and he soon attracted large crowds to Mission and Gospel Halls, especially when recounting his conversion story.

> 'As for me, my feet were almost gone', Ps 73v2.
> - 'almost in eternity without the Saviour'
> From Harold's conversion story

He became a member of the Christian Brethren fellowship in Ballymena, and in 1945, aged 21, was recognised by them as an evangelist, being formally 'commended to the Lord's work'. His fruitful preaching ministry was to span more than 60 years on four continents, and bears ample testimony to the good judgement of the elders of his church in 1945.

Some of his early preaching missions had great impact. One memorable series in Cregagh St Gospel Hall, Belfast, in 1947 saw many converted to Christ. Another in Rosslea, Co Fermanagh, undertaken

Young evangelist

with the encouragement of Dr Thomas Hagan and local RUC Sergeant John Thompson, saw the remarkable conversion of two RUC officers, both of whom went on to become significant Christian leaders. There were many more examples of the effect of the vibrant preaching of the young airman turned evangelist, and his ministry was soon in high demand.

Harold had no formal theological training or denominational ordination, as was consistent with the practice of the Christian Brethren. The nature of his ministry reflects the strong element of lay activism which has been their defining characteristic. He also belonged to a diminishing group of Christian workers who received no set salary and who learned to 'live by faith'.

Harold and Rosetta lived for periods of time in Belfast, Ballymena and Bangor. They had four children, Kenneth, Ruth, Harold and Linda. The family eventually grew to include two sons-in-law, Alastair and David, two daughters-in-law, Anne and Sharon, seven grandchildren, Douglas, Rosalyn, Kyle, David, Mark, Megan and Joshua, four grandchildren-in-law, Alice, John, Meredith and Tracy, and two great-grandchildren, Keziah and Daniel.

Two Decades of Ministry in Ulster

From 1945 to 1966, Harold Paisley became a well-known itinerant evangelist in Northern Ireland. In that period it is probably not an exaggeration to say that there was scarcely a Gospel Hall in the province where he did not conduct at least one series of Gospel

Belfast Tent, 1960s

Meetings. Some of these were high profile events including Tent Campaigns in Ballymena and Belfast. In the latter case, during the emerging tension in Ulster in the 1960s, his marquee in Belfast was burned down, perhaps because his evangelism was confused with the political activities of his brother Ian. While the two brothers were close and shared the same Christian faith, Harold had no connection with his brother's church or politics.

It is also safe to say that in this period there was hardly a Brethren church in Ulster which did not receive converts from Harold Paisley's preaching. These included families of existing members of the Brethren as well as a substantial number of adults who had no connection with the Gospel Hall. In addition, many of the existing Christians found new joy and confidence in their faith. Over the years, some fifteen of those who trusted Christ through Harold's ministry became evangelists or missionaries in the mould of their spiritual father.

In addition to Gospel preaching, Harold increasingly became a respected Bible Teacher. This was in an era when it was generally accepted that this form of ministry was the preserve of more experienced preachers. Harold brought into his Bible Teaching the same direct clarity and enthusiasm which characterised his Gospel preaching.

Preaching the Gospel under canvas

Forty five years of ministry in Canada and the US

In 1956-7, Harold spent a year with his family in Canada and the USA. He travelled extensively from coast to coast, conducting Gospel meetings and giving Bible teaching in Brethren assemblies and special conferences. Repeated invitations to visit Canada and the USA led to the family finally deciding to move permanently to Canada in 1966. They settled first in Toronto, then moved to Vancouver, and after some years returned to Toronto.

Canadian Family 1970

From 1966 until around 2010, Harold travelled extensively across Canada and the USA, preaching and teaching within the network of Gospel Halls. The strength of his ministry was undiminished, with many converts and great acceptance among a widening circle of Brethren churches. Some of his missions, such as those in Toronto, Vancouver, Boston, Iowa and Washington State, had high visibility and impact.

> *The white gulls above made us thankful again for safe journeys by land and sea during the last ten months and over 22,000 miles, among mountains, through forests, over prairies, through cities and over water and seas'.*
> **Personal diary, Jan 1957**

In his later years, Harold Paisley continued to be a highly respected evangelist and increasingly became a 'senior statesman' of the conservative Brethren in North America. He was, for example, a regular contributor to the Toronto and Vancouver Annual Bible Conferences.

At the Cottage

Harold valued his private and family life and found in them the relaxation and renewal his public commitments required. A small fishing hut at Six Mile Lake in Muskoka, Ont, was purchased by Etta in 1978 and developed over the years into a family retreat where children and grandchildren found great delight in outdoor activities. Harold enjoyed fishing, Etta organised fixing, and both found relaxation in the company of their family members and friends. 'The cottage' became a special place for the family.

In 2005, his commending assembly in Ballymena, Northern Ireland, now Cambridge Avenue Gospel Hall, held a celebratory evening to mark the 60th anniversary of his Gospel ministry. A number who had been greatly influenced by his ministry paid moving tributes to his impact on their lives.

The intensity of his travels and ministry began to diminish in the early 21st century, until in his mid-80s he effectively retired from public activity. His retirement years were spent with his wife and members of his family in Barrie, Ontario, Canada.

Visible Evangelism in Canada

In 2014, Harold and Rosetta, now long-time Canadian citizens, celebrated their 90th birthdays and, in 2015, 69 years of marriage. Their strong faith in Christ sustained them both through a time of declining physical and mental health. Their undiminished faith in a time of significant adversity underlined the authenticity of their commitment to Christ and His kingdom.

A Wider Ministry

Harold travelled extensively, both from Northern Ireland and from Canada. He led Gospel Missions in various parts of the UK, including one in Bristol, England, and on two notable occasions in canvas marquees in Glasgow, Scotland. One series of Gospel meetings in the Scottish town of Peterhead in 1963 had an echo of the revivals of a previous era in the fishing communities of NE Scotland.

Bellahouston Park, Glasgow, Scotland, 1992

He also travelled internationally, including visits to Australia, New Zealand, South Africa and Oman, to undertake evangelism and Bible teaching with Brethren congregations.

His Legacy

Harold Paisley's ministry as an evangelist and Bible teacher lies within the mainstream of conservative Open Brethren practice. By any

Seneca College Series, Toronto

measure, his contribution was outstanding, perhaps unsurpassed, in these circles.

He was not an innovator in evangelistic strategy, but operated with great effect within the norms of Brethren practice as he found it. His preaching was thoroughly orthodox, accepting the full authority of the Bible and declaring the foundational truths of the Christian faith. He also displayed a genuine personal commitment to the service of Christ and of others.

His evangelistic preaching was Biblical and direct, emphasising the need for personal repentance for sin and unconditional faith in the sacrifice of Jesus Christ for salvation. That reflected his personal experience of conversion. His style of preaching was compelling and carried great authority.

His 'Gospel Meetings' or 'Gospel Series' frequently lasted for several weeks and were often held in neutral venues such as canvas marquees or public halls. In the course of his ministry, he conducted a total of 70 'tent missions' in Ulster, Scotland, Canada and the USA. He often preached along with a colleague, including some well-known evangelists such as Tom Campbell and Tom Wallace (Northern Ireland), Joe Milne (Venezuela), Tom Bentley (Malaysia), and Oliver Smith and Norman Crawford (USA). His capacity to draw crowds was exceptional for a Brethren evangelist, and his meetings frequently had audiences in the hundreds and occasionally thousands. Over the years, the numbers of people professing faith were significant and over his lifetime ran into many hundreds.

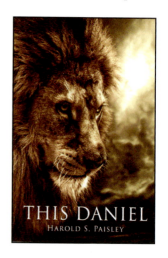

He was also in high demand among Brethren for his Bible teaching

> *'It is of great personal interest to me that John Cennick wrote: 'Brethren let us join to bless Jesus Christ, our joy and peace' in the village of Gracehill, Northern Ireland. James Montgomery also wrote many of his beautiful hymns there, and planted a tree still growing in the village square. For it was in Gracehill that I first met my wife, who grew up in the village, and who has been a great help to me in writing this book, as in all my Christian ministry over many years'.*
>
> **Preface to The Believers Hymn Book Companion**

and was a regular contributor to major conference events. His content was always imaginative, clear and personal. Some of his teaching became the subject of articles in Brethren magazines, particularly the Canadian publication 'Truth and Tidings'.

Harold is the author of several books, most of which feature prominent Bible characters. It gave Rosetta much pleasure to dedicate a recent reprint of his book *This Daniel* to his great-grandson Daniel who was born in 2014.

He also wrote about the background to the hymns in the Believers Hymn Book which is much used among the Brethren and which includes many of the great hymns of the Christian Faith.

Harold is also remembered by many for his thoughtful and effective pastoral support. Throughout his travels, he visited homes and hospitals to bring comfort and encouragement to those who were unwell or under pressure. He was also much in demand to conduct weddings and funeral services.

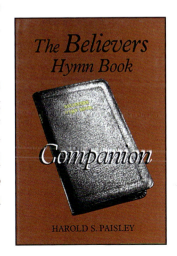

If Harold's role was that of preacher, Rosetta was the homemaker. Often in challenging circumstances, her tireless care of her family ensured that they had the domestic security to pursue their chosen educational and career paths. Her unfailing attention to family devotions helped to sustain the faith of her children.

Harold and Rosetta's family, with one exception, settled in Canada. Kenneth became a doctor, Harold a chiropractor and Linda a nurse. Ruth, who trained in Canada, became a primary school teacher and married in Scotland. Their extended families are now widespread and continue to contribute to the life of the Church in various settings. They still carry with them the strong personal faith in Jesus Christ as Lord and Saviour which so characterised the ministry of Harold Paisley.

In 2010, Harold's brother, the late Dr Ian R K Paisley MP MLA MEP and later Lord Bannside, provided a Foreword to the book *This Jesus*. He wrote: 'I welcome my beloved and only brother Harold's book as it adds yet another flower of sweet meditation to cast at the pierced feet of our Blessed Lord. … The delight of this book is that it leads us to hold the feet of the Saviour and glues us to His most precious face, both of which are sprinkled with His redeeming precious blood. It draws from our lips John Wesley's words,

Dr Ian RK Paisley, Lord Bannside

> Happy if with my latest breath
> I may but speak His name.
> Preach Him in life and cry in death,
> Behold, behold the Lamb!'

'Now I would desire to write about the Perfect Man – This Jesus. He is the sinless Saviour: "The Son of God who loved me and gave Himself for me" (Gal 2v20). The man who changed my life 66 years ago and who, since then, I have tried to serve. He has been my friend all these years, and I can assure you that, if you trust Him as your Saviour, He will never forsake you.

I dedicate 'This Jesus' to our four children and seven grandchildren. Especially Keziah Rose, our first great grandchild and pray that they may all love and serve The Lord Christ.'

Harold S Paisley, 2010

Obituary

Harold Paisley passed away peacefully on December 4th 2015 at Victoria Village Care Home in Barrie, Ontario, Canada. The funeral service in Barrie on December 12th was led by Michael Da Silva, with contributions from various members of the family. Several hundred attended, with friends and representatives from churches across Canada and the USA. Many spoke of the impact of Mr Paisley's ministry on their lives.

His death attracted comment in the Northern Ireland press, both in the *Belfast Telegraph* and the *News Letter*, noting the connection with his late brother Ian, the former First Minister of the province. One Canadian commentator in *BarrieToday.com* described Harold as 'a captivating and fiery preacher' and quoted a source who suggested he was 'the Billy Graham of the Plymouth Brethren'!

Harold Spurgeon Paisley is now 'at home with the Lord' (2 Cor 5v8).

Memories

*Margaret Beggs
Harold's sister*

In Proverbs 22 v6, the Bible says, *'Train up a child in the way he should go and when he is old he will not depart from it.* Certainly this verse proved to be true in the case of my brother Harold.

I was just three years old when war broke out in 1939 and that year Harold ran away from home to join the RAF – so of course I cannot remember his school days. However, there are many stories of how boisterous and mischievous he was, for example ringing people's door bells and running away, leaving his younger brother Ian to face the consequences!

One of my earliest memories was of Harold coming home on leave. How glad we were to see him, but we were also saddened by the fact that he was apparently far away from God. Then he would return to his unit, leaving our parents with a heavy heart. Eventually he was discharged from the RAF when it was discovered he was underage.

At that point he joined the Merchant Navy and on one occasion was posted missing when the activity of the German U Boats were at their worst in the North Atlantic. I have vivid memories of my mother pacing up and down our landing praying fervently, 'Lord save my boy'. She thought she would never see him again, but she longed to see him converted. Harold came home eventually and, having left the navy, joined the Royal Ulster Constabulary. While he was there he met some Christians whose testimony and lives made a deep impression on him.

Harold's dramatic conversion in Belfast in 1944 soon became widely known and gave joy and encouragement to many, but most especially to our family. What a change there was in his life! It was soon evident that he was really born again and he began to serve the Lord in public ministry, eventually joining the Brethren Assembly which met in the Gospel Hall in Ballymena and becoming an evangelist.

As a family we rejoice greatly that he has been instrumental in leading many souls to Christ over a long life and fruitful ministry. The thrust of his ministry can be summarised well in the words of the Apostle Paul: *'For I determined not to know anything among you, save Jesus Christ, and Him crucified'* (1 Cor. 2.2).

At a family wedding, 1989

Tommy McMullan
Northern Ireland

It is a pleasure for me to record some personal memories of my great friend Harold Paisley. He was a very remarkable man who lived out what he believed and preached. One of the most gifted communicators I have heard, he spoke with softness and sincerity, both in gospel preaching and Bible teaching. He saw a great many people come to know the Lord and his teaching was always a great encouragement to the Christians who came to his meetings.

I attended many of the series of gospel meetings he held in Northern Ireland and was greatly blessed through them. I have vivid memories of these occasions to which large numbers of the people came. In Ballymena, for example, a large 5-pole marquee with seating for almost 1000 was filled every evening, and on some nights several hundred people had to stand outside. Another series of meetings, held in the centre of Ballymena on a vacant site at Morton's Mill, had Harold and missionary Tom Bentley as the preachers, with audiences of up to 800. A more recent innovation was a 'drive in' open air format behind Ballymena Fire Station where many heard Harold preach from a platform erected on the back of a lorry.

I remember in the 1960s a memorable series of gospel meetings in the centre of Belfast, held in a marquee with seating for 1000 which was erected on a vacant site. These attracted large crowds, and significant numbers of those who heard the gospel there came to trust the Lord Jesus. The following year, the meetings in the marquee were repeated, though on this occasion it was burned down, creating a news story and giving significant publicity to the evangelistic work being done. The last meeting of that series was held on a Sunday evening in the Ulster Hall.

Although Harold frequently preached to large crowds in tents and portable halls in major centres, he was also committed to preaching the gospel across rural Ulster in Gospel Halls and other public venues. Regardless of the size of the audience, Harold Paisley never wavered in his forthright declaration of the gospel. Few evangelists I have known preached with such conviction and to such great effect. It has been an honour for me to have known him.

....

Mike Da Silva
Toronto, Canada

I'm so privileged to write a short account of my encounter with a man whose knowledge of God was deeply personal. I was born and raised in the city of Toronto, Canada, the son of Portuguese immigrant parents.

My wife Kathy had a work friend who invited us regularly to come to her church, Bracondale Gospel Hall, Toronto, but I was not inclined to go as I was, at least nominally, a Roman Catholic.

However, on Sunday 16th December 1984, Mr Paisley was due to preach there and she invited us again. This time we accepted. I listened to Mr Paisley preach the Gospel and after the meeting on my way out I had a remarkable conversation with him. As we chatted, he asked me directly, 'Where will you spend eternity?' My answer was simply, 'I don't know' and, as he patiently took me through a number of passages from the Bible, he led me to a personal faith in Jesus Christ as my Lord and Saviour.

Our close friendship has continued for over 30 years and I was privileged to share the preaching with him in many series of gospel meetings in the greater Toronto area. I also had the joy of travelling with him to Ireland, Britain and the USA. As Mr Paisley began to age, he travelled less but still enjoyed visiting smaller local churches in order to encourage them in their Christian life and witness.

As a result of knowing Mr Paisley, over a dozen members of my family have come to know Christ and the blessing of the gospel in their lives. I am sure my story is only one of many thousands from people who came to know this man of God.

· · · · · · · · ·

Philip Johnston, Bangor, NI

Harold Paisley was a unique man and I look back to my youth and his influence on my own coming to faith. I well remember the night he clarified the gospel in my mind when he said he was not depending on the strength of his own faith but simply in the surety of what Christ had done for him. We all owe a debt to men and women of his calibre and I look forward to meeting him again in heaven as the one who pointed me to The Lord!

· · · · · · · · ·

*Ashley Milne
Vancouver, Canada*

I remember the first time I met Harold Paisley in 1958. I was sixteen years old and my parents, Joe and Georgina Milne, and family had just returned from Venezuela for a spell in Northern Ireland. When my parents returned to Venezuela, Mr Paisley promised that he would keep an eye on me, which he did during the ensuing years. Many years later, my wife and I were privileged to have him as a guest in our home in Vancouver. He took a real interest in our son, Alistair, as he did with many young men, and would often stay up late to talk to him about the Bible - just as he had done with me in previous years. Many will look back and consider him instrumental in bringing them to faith in Christ; others of us remember him as an outstandingly gifted teacher!

Wedding Day 1946

*Harold and Rosetta Paisley
1980s*

Publications by Harold Paisley

The Gospel of Mark in *What the Bible Teaches*, Vol 1, Ritchie 1984
The Person of Christ, various chapters therein, Gospel Tract Publications, 1987
The Believers Hymn Book Companion, Gospel Tract Publications, 1989
This Daniel, Essential Truth Publishers, Illinois. 1972, reprinted Olive Press 1991
This Ruth, Olive Press, 1995
This Joseph, Olive Press, 2002
This Jesus, Gospel Folio Press, Ont, 2010

> 'It is the desire and prayer of the present writer that all of us may walk in fellowship with God, with devotedness of heart to our Glorious Redeemer and with a greater love for the Holy Scriptures.'
>
> *This Daniel, p198*